If I Only Knew . . .

What Would Jesus Do?

for Women

Over 100 Ways to "Walk the Walk" and "Talk the Talk"

Joan Hake Robie

STARBURST PUBLISHERS®
Lancaster, Pennsylvania

To schedule Author appearances write: Author Appearances, Starburst Promotions, P.O. Box 4123, Lancaster, Pennsylvania 17604 or call (717) 293-0939. Web site: www.starburstpublishers.com

CREDITS:
Cover design by David Marty Design
Text design and composition by John Reinhardt Book Design

Unless otherwise noted, or paraphrased by the author, all Scripture quotations are from the New International Version of The Holy Bible.

"Scripture taken from the HOLY BIBLE: NEW INTERNATIONAL VERSION®. NIV®. Copyright © 1973, 1978, 1984 by International Bible Society. Used by permission of Zondervan Publishing House."

"The 'NIV' and 'New International Version' trademarks are registered in the United States Patent and Trademark Office by International Bible Society."

To the best of its ability, Starburst Publishers® has strived to find the source of all material. If there has been an oversight, please contact us and we will make any correction deemed necessary in future printings. We also declare that to the best of our knowledge all material (quoted or not) contained herein is accurate, and we shall not be held liable for the same.

IF I ONLY KNEW... WHAT WOULD JESUS DO? FOR WOMEN

First Printing, May 1999

ISBN: 0-892016-087
Library of Congress Catalog Number 98-83168
Printed in the United States of America

What Would Jesus Do for Women

Introduction

*And the rib, which the LORD God had taken from man, made he a **woman** . . . .*
GENESIS 2:22 (KJV)

Women are unique—so unlike their male counterparts. They are different physically, mentally, emotionally, socially, and spiritually.

So far as likes and dislikes are concerned, if you were to take a poll on how many men like to shop—especially at malls, you would come up with very few.

Or how many women would enjoy a week or more on a wilderness trip in a remote area of the country, where your last fifty miles of driving is on a dirt road? Leaving your vehicle parked at a lodge (the only building for miles around), you transport (by foot) your canoe, with food, clothing, and shelter (tent) from lake to lake. There will be no telephone and almost no human contact for the duration of your trip.

As you read *WHAT WOULD JESUS DO?*, which I've written with the woman in mind, put yourself into each life experience, much of which is based on fact, and decide for yourself what Jesus would do.

Other Books by Starburst Publishers

(Partial listing—full list available on request)

If I Only Knew What Jesus Would Do? for Women   —Joan Hake Robie
Finally a *WWJD?* just for women! This book, a follow-up to the successful *If I Only I Knew . . . WWJD?* offers women special guidance from Jesus' perspective.

(trade paper)   ISBN 1892016087   **$9.95**

God's Abundance   —Edited by Kathy Collard Miller
Let God's Word lead you to a simpler, yet more abundant life in this day-to-day inspirational. Learn to make all aspects of your life a "spiritual abundance of simplicity."

(cloth)   ISBN 0914984977   **$19.95**

God's Unexpected Blessings   —Edited by Kathy Collard Miller
Witness God at work in our lives to see the *unexpected blessings* of our most challenging experiences, as God turns all things for our good.

(cloth)   ISBN 0914984071   **$18.95**

Seasons of a Woman's Heart—
A Daybook of Stories and Inspiration   —Compiled by Lynn D. Morrissey
Christian writers, such Kay Arthur, Emilie Barnes, Luci Swindoll, Jill Briscoe, and Florence Littauer, offer inspiring thoughts on the seasons of a woman's heart.

(cloth)   ISBN 1892016036   **$18.95**

More of Him, Less of Me   —Jan Christensen
This yearlong daybook of inspiration will encourage you on your weight-loss journey. Perfect companion guide for anyone on the Weigh Down™ diet!

(cloth)   ISBN 1892016001   **$17.95**

PURCHASING INFORMATION:
www.starburstpublishers.com

Books are available from your favorite bookstore, either from current stock or special order. To assist bookstore in locating your selection be sure to give title, author, and ISBN #. If unable to purchase from the bookstore, you may order direct from STARBURST PUBLISHERS. When ordering, enclose full payment plus shipping and handling as follows: Post Office (4th Class)—$3.00 (Up to $20.00), $4.00 ($20.01-$50.00), 8% ($50.01 and Up); UPS—$4.50 (Up to $20.00), $6.00 ($20.01-$50.00), 12% ($50.01 and Up); Canada—$5.00 (Up to $35.00), 15% ($35.01 and Up); Overseas (Surface)—$5.00 (Up to $25.00), 20% ($25.01 and Up). Payment in U.S. Funds only. Please allow two to three weeks minimum (longer overseas) for delivery. Make checks payable to and mail to: STARBURST PUBLISHERS, P.O. Box 4123, LANCASTER, PA 17604. Credit card orders may also be placed by calling 1-800-441-1456 (credit card orders only), Mon-Fri, 8:30 a.m. to 5:30 p.m. Eastern Standard Time. Prices subject to change without notice. Catalog available for a 9 x 12 self-addressed envelope with 4 first-class stamps.

What Would Jesus Do for Women

About Women Role Models?

For years women have been looked upon as the ones who held up the banner of morality in the home—who nurtured their children, teaching them the ways of God and right living—all the while a large majority of their husbands rejected any personal allegiance to God or the church.

For example, take the popular TV sitcom of a few years ago—*All In The Family* starring Archie Bunker and wife. Edith was a dutiful prim-and-proper church-goer while Archie was a staunch critic of her standards as well as society in general.

Today, however, thanks to organizations like *Promise Keepers* and others, many men are taking the leadership of the home and family very seriously. They are putting their households in order and being the spiritual head of the family. What can a woman do to encourage her husband to follow the ways of righteousness?

Think about it . . .

MATTHEW 15:28 (NIV)

*Then Jesus answered, "Woman, you have great faith!
Your request is granted." . . .*

It seems that women in general have always had a heart for the Lord. Perhaps it may be as a result of their *mothering* that this has come about. Men were the hunters and providers of the daily sustenance for the family, so, it was up to the women to teach the children, not only about life, but also about spiritual things. In Luke 10:39 we read . . . *She had a sister called Mary, who sat at the Lord's feet listening to what he said.* We should follow her example.

About a Woman's Gift of Love?

Today's society seems to interpret the word L O V E as the giving of material things and/or sex. Rarely is love interpreted as "one giving one's *all* for another."

Never was love put to the test as it was with John Williams and his wife Lorraine. John was a successful entrepreneur until he needed a kidney transplant.

As it turned out, Lorraine was a perfect match and eager to risk her life by giving a kidney so that her husband could live. Only John and Lorraine can tell you how this experience has drawn them closer together—true, love conquers all!

Meditate . . .

WWJD?

Song of Solomon 4:7 (NIV)

How beautiful you are, my darling; there is no flaw in you.

When Lorraine's husband needed a kidney donor and she learned that she was a match she didn't think twice about it before saying yes. She loved her husband so much that she was willing to pay any price for his life. That's what Jesus did for us—he gave his life so that we can have eternal life. What a sacrifice!

With a Consecrated Woman?

When Mary accepted the Lord as her Savior her life was completely changed. No longer did she spend her weekends "hanging out at the sports bar." She became a "new creature in Christ" and her old life passed away. She now longed for fellowship with her Lord Jesus Christ and Christian friends rather than her old friends at the bar.

"Mary's got religion!" they laughed at the bar. "She's not having fun anymore."

But Mary knew all to well that the "fun" they spoke of was nothing to be compared with the joy she now has with her Lord . . . and the joy of the Lord doesn't leave her with a hangover!

Think about . . .

II Corinthians 5:17 (NIV)

*Therefore, if anyone is in Christ, he is a new creation;
the old has gone, the new has come!*

The ways of the world have a high price, and it does not last.
The joy found in serving Christ lasts forever. This is what Jesus
would do—give us joy!

When a Baby Has His Way?

"Blessed Event" it's called when a newborn baby arrives on the scene. But the sacrifices a mother and father have to make for the little one drastically changes the family's schedule.

Take, for example, the times when baby has been bathed and is all dressed to go out. You take inventory of all the supplies you need—bottles, diapers, wet wipes, etc. Then, just as you go out the door you smell something—it's time for another change. What do you do? You either turn around and go back inside the house and bathe baby all over again and stay home. Or, you go out late—after baby is ready again.

Imagine . . .

ROMANS 15:4 (NIV)
For everything that was written in the past was written to teach us, so that through endurance and the encouragement of the Scriptures we might have hope.

Babies certainly do have their way, not always as in the example given here, but in many other ways. Baby has his way when he needs a bottle, or to be held. Sometimes a parent is very tired from all he or she has done throughout the day. But, baby comes first—we need to learn the patience to deal with all the variables that come along with this "blessed event!" This is what Jesus would do.

About Loving Parents?

"Daddy's hugging mommy again," announces six-year-old Bobby to his two siblings—four-year-old Betsy and two-year-old Patty.

"Me, too," squeals Betsy as she runs toward her parents, little Patty at her heels.

"Up," calls Patty as her father lifts her up next to him and his wife Joanna.

"Come over here, Bobby," says his father warmly, "You're not too old to be hugged."

Practically grownup Bobby gives in and with a smile joins in on the "family hug."

The occasion was an ordinary day in the life of this family—one where father and mother love each other as well as their children. Not without its daily challenges, their home is dedicated to the Lord and each other; and the children are secure in that love.

Consider . . .

Ephesians 5:25 (NIV)

Husbands, love your wives, just as Christ loved the church and gave himself up for her . . . .

The family here is one that is built on love. The husband and wife love one another as well as their children. With Christ at the head of their home, they have the secret for a happy life.

To "Baby Proof" a House?

"What a beautifully-decorated house you have, Mrs. Conover," remarked young wife and mother Jean Brady, "and all the fine crystal and art pieces—how do you keep everything looking so luxurious? My house has so much clutter . . . with the babies and all."

"Well, Jean," replied Mrs. Conover, " before we had children we had a little 'dream' cottage—but when the children came along I soon learned to *baby proof* the house—remove all or nearly all knickknacks and unnecessary clutter that was sitting around on tables and bookshelves. Things that were waiting to be knocked to the floor and get broken. Knickknacks and other collectibles were put away in boxes and clutter was not allowed to accumulate. In other words, I went 'back to the basics' in my house decorations. Now that the children are no longer little and living at home, I can enjoy the knickknacks and finer things again. But they do not 'control' me—I can live with them or without them."

Decide . . .

WWJD?

HEBREWS 12:1 (NIV)

Therefore, since we are surrounded by such a great cloud of witnesses, let us throw off everything that hinders and the sin that so easily entangles, and let us run with perseverance the race marked out for us.

There are so many things in life that can weigh us down. Preoccupation with material things such as fine furniture, crystal and/or collectibles can cause them to become a burden rather than a blessing. Simplicity and efficiency is the best policy during the years of raising a family. Easily-cleaned kitchen surfaces are the best choice. Fine crystal, art pieces, and knick-knacks can be displayed after the children have grown up.

What Would Jesus Do for Women

About a Single-Parent Home?

"I wish Daddy lived with us," complained Mark, "he would let me watch what I want on TV."

"Well, your daddy doesn't live here anymore, so I'm in charge—you'll do as *I* say," returned his mother Elaine in desperation.

Disgruntled, Mark stomped up the stairs to his bedroom. Then he sat at his desk looking out the window at the sunset.

"Why can't I have a daddy who lives with us?" Mark thought. "We used to have a lot of fun before he left us. Why can't he come back?" he cried, the tears running down his cheeks.

Consider . . .

MATTHEW 12:25 (NIV)

*. . . every city or household divided against itself will
  not stand.*

Mark's story is not unlike that of other children who feel the
heartache of a broken home—children whose daddy or mother
no longer lives with them. Our Lord draws near to these precious ones to wipe away their tears and comfort them.

About a Cluttered House?

Why is it that some people can dress "fit for a king" and yet live in a hovel? Their clothes are spotless—every hair on their head is in place and a smile is on their face—when they go out. But "back at the ranch" (their house) the bathroom shows all the signs of their getting dressed—towels on the floor, hairbrushes full of hair, makeup and toiletries scattered about, dirty tub and sink, and the clothes they took off dropped on the floor just where they stepped out of them. The rest of the house looks the same—a cluttered "mess!"

Ask . . .

PSALM 8:3 (NIV)

When I consider your heavens, the work of your fingers, the moon and the stars, which you have set in place,

Our God believes in "order." This was proven during Creation when He put everything in its place (order). Then, too, the Garden of Eden was a beauty to behold— trees, plants, fruit and flowers all balanced for optimum growth and beauty (order). This is how God wants us to live our lives (in order). Likewise, we should keep our house clean, with everything in its place; if it drops, pick it up; if you can't use it, get rid of it!

Getting rid of your "clutter," both physically and spiritually, is the beginning of gaining control of your life.

About a Too-Busy Mom?

"Mom, help me with my homework—this math assignment is too hard." moaned Jennifer.

"Please," returned her mom.

"Please," complied Jennifer with exasperation.

"I'd like to help you, Jennifer, but you know how busy I am ever since your dad left us. I'm only one person, you know. . . get Billy to help you—he's older and knows more about math than I do."

"Oh, OK, but I know Billy won't have time either—he's always talking on the telephone with his girlfriend," retorted Jennifer.

"Well, at least ask him," sighed her mother as she rushed about doing the laundry.

Consider . . .

MATTHEW 23:37 (NIV)

. . . how often I have longed to gather your children together, as a hen gathers her chicks under her wings, but you were not willing.

Time spent with our children is quality time. Not having a husband around makes it more difficult for Jennifer's mother. But if she does not *make time* to help her children with their projects such as homework she will regret it later. The growing-up years are precious—we cannot reclaim them once they're gone. Jesus would agree.

To Teach Us to Stand on Our Own?

Growing up, we learn to take risks on our own (just as a baby takes steps and then looks back to see if the parent is watching). But in spite of a baby's freedom of discovery, he or she needs to be within the reach of someone who can help should the babyfall down.

A young woman becoming a homemaker needs a parent or other person to call upon when the cake "falls" or when the potatoes get lumpy. At what point do we begin to analyze a problem and stand on our own? Doesn't that depend on the rate of our maturity? Of course it does. What do you do when someone never seems to develop beyond a certain point?

Think about . . .

I Corinthians 13:11 (NIV)
When I was a child, I talked like a child, I thought like a child, I reasoned like a child. When I became a man, I put childish ways behind me.

Personal discovery is a part of maturity. Jesus spent many hours by the sea teaching his disciples. He encouraged them to learn on their own—not to be totally dependent on Him. For example, rather than lecturing the disciples on what they should learn, Jesus sometimes spoke in parables and even wrote in the sand. He wants us to use our minds and bodies to the fullest. That often means taking risks on our own.

To Press Toward the Mark?

"You can make it!"

Did you ever have someone in your life who encouraged you to press on to reach your goals? One who would not just "give advice," but would praise you for each step you take? Perhaps it was a spiritual leader who asked you to assist in children's church. Or it may have been a music teacher who motivated you to practice your instrument.

I'll never forget the pastor of my church when I was a teenager. He was forever encouraging his parishioners, especially the youth of the church, to use their talents for the Lord. Even if that talent was not developed to a place of "professionalism," they were encouraged to participate. Pastor saw it as a ministry unto the Lord—not a performance for Carnegie Hall. (Selah)

"You can make it!" goes a long way to bring success into someone's life.

Envision . . .

PHILIPPIANS 3:14 (NIV)
. . . I press on toward the goal to win the prize for which
God has called me heavenward in Christ Jesus.

Isn't it pleasant to be around someone who encourages you in your endeavors and praises you for your successes? The Apostle Paul encouraged his followers to "press toward the mark."

That's what Jesus would do.

To Save a Life?

"You saved my life, Dale," commented Dennis to his friend as they walked home from school.

"What do you mean —saved your life?"

"Remember when we first met and you helped me home with my schoolbooks and other stuff from my locker?"

"Yes."

"Well, that day I was at my end—trouble in school, trouble at home—it was a mess. So I was planning to commit suicide. Then you came along and showed me that somebody cared about me."

"Wow!" responded Dale with enthusiasm, "do you really mean that?"

"I sure do! You saved my life!"

Recall . . .

I Thessalonians 4:9 (NIV)
*Now about brotherly love we do not need to write to
you, for you yourselves have been taught by God to
love each other.*

Dale's mother, Esther, was at home alone the day that Dale
first met Dennis. She was praying for her son, that God would
keep him on the right path—just as she did every day. "Lord,"
she prayed, "help my son to be a blessing to his classmates
today." Little did she realize the impact of that prayer.

About a Woman's Forgiveness?

The summer of 1998 brought to light one of our country's biggest scandals of the century—that of President Bill Clinton who, after much pressure, admitted that he had been unfaithful to his wife, Hillary, and deceptive to his nation. The tabloids kept pumping out news of the scandal on a daily basis. Finally, upon being forced "against the wall," the President first lied about the scandal, then made public confession to the nation and his wife that he had a liaison with a young woman.

Hillary Rodham Clinton is thought by some to be like the *Rock of Gibraltar*—immoveable! She appears to let nothing stand in the way of her faithful support of her husband. But will her husband's unfaithfulness be enough to break up the marriage?

Answer the question . . .

PROVERBS 12:2 (NIV)
*A good man obtains favor from the LORD, but the
LORD condemns a crafty man.*

Only time will tell how the President's wife has endured being made a public spectacle. Only time will tell if the marriage will survive such an onslaught. But one thing is for sure—Jesus is willing to forgive and forget what President Bill Clinton has done—just as He forgives and forgets our sins if we confess them and ask forgiveness!

About Cleansing the Mind?

Turn on the TV—and what are you likely to see?—lustful behavior, infidelity, lying, stealing, hatred, profanity, violence, and death!

Go to a movie—and what are you likely to see (even in PG13 films)?— lustful behavior, infidelity, lying, stealing, profanity, violence, and death!

The same goes for many of today's periodicals, especially magazines, videos, and CDs.

It's no wonder that our minds are filled with all kinds of ungodly thoughts that are acted out in many lives. What can we do?

Face the issue . . .

PHILIPPIANS 4:8 (NIV)

Finally, brothers, whatever is true, whatever is noble, whatever is right, whatever is pure, whatever is lovely, whatever is admirable—if anything is excellent or praiseworthy—think about such things.

Recently we went to a movie that the ticket salesperson said was rated **PG** and was very "funny"—however, while walking down the hallway to the movie (after we'd gotten our tickets, and popcorn and drink) we saw a sign above us listing the movie as PG 13. Still thinking that the movie would be acceptable and very "funny" we went in and sat down.

But to our "horror"—from the very beginning, the movie was nothing but violence, profanity, and death!

As the minutes went on our spirits grew more and more disturbed . . .

"Let's get out of this awful place!" I said, resolving never to sit at the "table of the evil one" again!

NOTE: Upon reporting the incident to the manager, we "got our money back!"

When a Wife Cries Out?

When I ask you to listen to me,
and you start giving me advice,
You have not done what I asked.
When I ask that you listen to me,
And you begin to tell me why
I shouldn't feel that way,
You are trampling on my feelings.

When I ask you to listen to me,
and you feel you have to do
something to solve my problems,
you have failed me, strange
as that may seem.
Listen: All that I ask is that
*   you listen,*
Not talk or do—just hear me.
When you do something for me
That I need to do for myself,

You contribute to my fear
and feelings of inadequacy.

But when you accept as a
simple fact
That I do feel what I feel, no
matter how irrational,
Then I can quit trying to
convince you

And go about the business
Of understanding what's be-
hind my feelings.
So please listen and just
hear me.
And if you want to talk,
Wait a minute for your turn
— and I'll listen to you.

Ponder . . .

LUKE 10:40 (NIV)

But Martha was distracted by all the preparations that had to be made. She came to him and asked, "Lord, don't you care that my sister has left me to do the work by myself? Tell her to help me!"

The art of listening—so often when we pray we seemingly "bombard" our Lord with the burdens that we carry and our "wants." Rarely do we "listen" to his voice and what he has to say to us. In the Scriptures we read how Mary was eager to learn from Jesus while Martha was busy with the household chores.

When Grown-ups Worry?

When asked the reason for longevity, one wrinkle-faced centenarian remarked, "I never was a worrier. I didn't let things get to me."

But, unlike this veteran of life's experiences, most people we know spend much of their time worrying about things that they can do nothing about. They worry about how their children are going to make it in life; how much money they'll earn, and if they'll be healthy.

Although worry is one of *nature's alarm systems,* it can also become overwhelming (toxic) and lead to the deterioration of one's physical health. So, how can you stop being a constant worrier?

Ask yourself . . .

WWJD?

MATTHEW 6:25 (NIV)

*Therefore I tell you, do not worry about your life, what
you will eat or drink; or about your body, what you
will wear. Is not life more important than food, and
the body more important than clothes?*

Are you a constant worrier—do you worry about almost everything? Then it's time to give your worry to the Lord—and receive his peace. This is what he is waiting to give you.

With a Hurting Spirit?

Recently my sister Wanda lost her husband John to a fatal disease. Although John had helped prepare Wanda for the time when she would be alone (selling their two older automobiles and purchasing one that would be reliable, building a room onto their house that Wanda could use for her in-home business, and making necessary house repairs), this would not prepare Wanda for the lonely hours when she would miss her beloved John. The times when she would wish that she were with him. Having to go places alone and feel like a displaced person, or going places with a married couple, or even with single ladies, only reinforced the hurt that didn't want to go away. What was she to do?

Ponder . . .

ECCLESIASTES 3:4 (KJV)

*A time to weep, and a time to laugh; a time to mourn,
and a time to dance;*

Were it not for the prayers of others and the hospice help-group that Wanda attended—where people like her were struggling to survive their loss, Wanda's hurting spirit would not release its hold on her life so she could be whole again. Would you agree that Wanda should also see old as well as new friends and get on with her life? This is undoubtedly what Jesus would want her to do.

When a Child Faces Reality?

"I want to see Poppy again,"cried four-year-old Jesse to his mother as she took his hand and the two of them walked across the vestibule of the church to where his grandfather lay in a coffin. As Jesse's mother held him up to see his beloved Poppy for the last time Jesse said, "I want to go to heaven with Poppy."

"Some day you will go to heaven and see Poppy—but not now. Jesus will let you know when that time comes."

Satisfied with his mother's answer, Jesse spied a drinking fountain near the front doorway of the church. "I'm thirsty!" he said.

Straightening the blue cotton, short-legged suit that Jesse wore, his mother put him down on the floor—his little legs running toward the fountain. As his mother held him up to the fountain, Jesse thirstily drank the bubbling water and said, "That's good!"

Meditate . . .

I Corinthians 15:52 (KJV)

*In a moment, in the twinkling of an eye, at the last
trump: for the trumpet shall sound, and the dead
shall be raised incorruptible, and we shall be changed.*

Although a child cannot understand the reality of death, he
or she can understand the spiritual side of it—that of going to
be with Jesus. When Jesse's mother explained that Poppy was
going to heaven, and that some day they would be reunited
with him, Jesse's heart was satisfied. Likewise, we, too, can have
that blessed hope—of seeing our loved ones once again.

About Children Doing Chores?

We have photographs of our two boys, Jonathan and Mark, one washing the dishes and the other sitting up on the kitchen counter drying and putting the dishes into the cabinets. The boys were only 9 and 12 years-old at the time, but they were expected to do everyday household chores just like the rest of the family.

Now the boys are grown and one of them is adept at cooking—especially at carving a turkey. The other, while not too excited about household chores, knows what has to be done.

Colonel Harland D. Sanders of *Kentucky Fried Chicken* fame baked his first loaf of bread when he was only five years-old. (His mother took in sewing—working long hours at a time, so the children had to take care of the household duties.) Colonel Sanders prided himself on his accomplishment of learning to bake and cook because it helped him gain experience in life and opened the door to his future chicken business success.

Consider . . .

PROVERBS 22:6 (KJV)

Train up a child in the way he should go: and when he is old, he will not depart from it.

It is good to teach children how to work. They will be happier and more fulfilled if they have regular responsibilities that they are assigned to—such as washing dishes, sweeping the floor, taking out the trash, minding smaller siblings, etc. This is what Jesus would do!

About Anger?

How often have you encountered someone who says or does something that conflicts with your belief system? Perhaps their upbringing and values are different from yours. This sense of unfairness caused *anger* to rise up within you. Suddenly you had a decision to make—to allow the anger to create stress within you or to let love and forgiveness drive out the anger. If you allow anger to grow in you it will turn into *resentment*. A solution to the problem cannot come so long as the anger is present.

Make your decision . . .

PROVERBS 29:22 (NIV)

*An angry man stirs up dissension, and a hot-tempered
one commits many sins.*

Try to find the source of your anger—think back into your
childhood—was it something that a parent or brother or sister
did to cause you to have this deep-seated anger? Once you've
found the cause, give it to the Lord and ask forgiveness for
allowing anger to possess you. Let Christ replace the anger with
love. This is what Jesus would do!

About Regrets?

Regrets! Regrets! Regrets!

It is doubtful that anyone who has ever walked this earth can say they've had no regrets in life.

Regrets come in all shapes and sizes, and the effect they have on an individual is borne out by the magnitude of the regret:

- Why didn't I keep the soapbox my son made for his competition in the derby?
- Why did I let my child have his own way?
- Why didn't I visit my mother more often at the nursing home?
- Why didn't I spend more time reading the Bible?

Why . . .

PHILIPPIANS 3:13 (KJV)
. . . forgetting those things which are behind, and reaching forth unto those things which are before,

Our Lord is willing to forgive and forget all our regrets. He asks only that we take these regrets to him in prayer, then leave them there . . . never to take them back again.

To Bring Trust to a Family?

How often are families dysfunctional due to a lack of trust in one another?

Take the Donald Spaulding family, for example—after their first child was born, Donald got a *vasectomy*. Five years later his wife became pregnant again.

"There's no way this could be my child!" Donald told his wife accusingly—"I had a vasectomy."

"But she *is* your daughter!" reasoned wife Mary.

For years a cloud of suspicion hung over the family . . . then, another child, a son, was born.

Think about . . .

PROVERBS 3:30 (NIV)

Do not accuse a man for no reason—when he has done you no harm.

"Your vasectomy became *undone*," explained the doctor to Mr. Spaulding, "this happens from time-to-time."

Upon hearing this, Mr. Spaulding was remorseful and asked his wife's forgiveness. The years of estrangement between this husband and wife now gave way to trust.

To Bring Joy to a Birthday Child?

"When are you going to open your gifts?" asked Bonnie excitedly to her friend Karen who was celebrating her birthday.

"My mother said we're going to open the gifts later—after the party is over," answered Karen dejectedly. "I asked her to please let me open them while my friends are here—but she said no."

Is this the trend taking place . . . that gifts given for birthdays, weddings, etc. are opened *after* the guests leave? If so, why is this being done?

Ask yourself . . .

I Timothy 6:18 (NIV)

. . . be generous and willing to share.

Both children and adults enjoy selecting a present, then wrapping it and writing a greeting card to go along with the gift. Just to watch a friend's face when he or she opens a gift is a delight to most guests. (A gift that is purchased, or even handmade, can be equally appreciated. So no one should feel that they have nothing to give.)

In addition, watching a friend open their gifts teaches patience, and giving, when others are being honored. This would bring joy to our Lord.

To Comfort a Disappointed Child?

World War II saw a significant number of changes on the home front. Not only did women have to don coveralls and work in defense plants, but underage children were hired to work in local shops and stores.

Eleven-year-old Ellen was one of those who applied for part-time work. It was at Kirsten's Stationery store. Wary of hiring such a young girl, yet realizing that it was difficult to find help in those days, Mr. Kirsten gave it a try.

After a few hours it was obvious to Mr. Kirsten that Ellen was too young for the job —when a customer asked for **REDBOOK** (magazine), Ellen went looking through the magazines for a red book. The last straw was Ellen's taking price tags off the greeting cards before tallying the cost of each card. Broken-hearted Ellen left the store without a job.

Consider . . .

I Thessalonians 5:14 (NIV)

And we urge you, brothers, warn those who are idle, encourage the timid, help the weak, be patient with everyone.

Ellen learned a lesson that one day on the job—at the school of hard knocks. The Lord Jesus would put his arms around this child to comfort her as she faced one of life's challenges. One thing for sure—Ellen will never forget the magazine called **REDBOOK!**

With a Job Left Undone?

We've all seen a child get out his toys but not want to put them away—even if the parent is willing to help him.

Of course, if the parent doesn't insist that the toys be put away they won't be, and the parent will have the chore after the child has gone to bed.

This should not be—a child should be taught, from little on up, that a job begun must be completed—in other words, toys gotten out must be put away. No amount of screaming and kicking should change the parent's mind. The child has to learn to obey. How is this done?

Decide . . .

PROVERBS 22:6 (KJV)
Train up a child in the way he should go: and when he is old, he will not depart from it.

One way to encourage a child to put away toys and other playthings is to assist him or her with the job. Then, little-by-little, back out and let the child do it by himself. You may wish to reward him with some little gift, possibly a cookie or the like. Soon you will have taught him the virtue of a job begun is a job well done and the child will learn to put his toys away without too much prompting. That's what Jesus would do.

What Would Jesus Do for Women

With a Wayward Teenager?

The BIG QUESTION? What do you do with wayward teenagers?
Here are some suggestions:

1. Keep them busy with lots of household chores (include some that they like).
2. Their social life must be with young people who are dedicated to the Lord.
3. When they go out, they must stay with the group.
4. "Ground" them, except for school, when they deliberately disobey.
5. Provide for pastoral counseling for them and the family as a whole.
6. Share ideas and "helps" with other parents.
7. Be an example of godliness before your teens–and above all *listen*.
8. Pray and intercede for the teens (yours and others).

Ask . . . .

PROVERBS 22:6 (KJV)

Train up a child in the way he should go: and when he is old, he will not depart from it.

The Word speaks for itself. Jesus agrees with the Word—the Scriptures. He would admonish parents to "walk-the-walk" and "talk-the-talk."

About Wearing "Jeans" to Church?

Why is it that certain professions expect their employees to dress up for work—tailored suits, dress shoes (higher heels preferred for women), yet a large number of today's church-goers jump out of bed and pull on jeans or even "shorts" to wear to church?

"It's not like going to the grocery store or to a ball game or shopping," said one pastor who asked his congregation to smarten up their Sunday dress. "It's a sign of respect and admiration."

Other pastors believe dress is not important. "I'd rather they come to church in jeans than not come at all." one commented.

What is your opinion on the subject? As a woman, do you feel more comfortable dressed up or in casual wear such as slacks or even jeans? Which of the pastors here do you agree with?

Better still . . .

I TIMOTHY 2:9 (NIV)

*I also want women to dress modestly, with decency
and propriety, not with braided hair or gold or pearls
or expensive clothes.*

If Jesus walked this earth today and was confronted with the
subject of dress, he would likely prefer a style of clothing that
would be in line with those of his age. If a teenager—perhaps
jeans would get the vote. If an adult—possibly dress-up clothes.
However, uppermost in His mind would be *modesty* and *to please
the Father*.

What Would Jesus Do for Women

To Make Us "Lighten-Up?"

Many churches of today are a "far cry" from those of yesterday. Instead of rigid liturgical services with the pastor wearing a turned collar and the formal garb of the "clergy," they stand before the congregation wearing the suit and tie of the business world (some even wear sportswear). Musical performances are honored with applause, and most of the songs are the recent work of young composers. The congregation stands for much of the worship—the clapping of hands is not uncommon. How should we worship?

Ask . . .

PSALM 100:1 (NIV)
. . . . *Shout for joy to the LORD, all the earth.*

True, today church worship is a lot different than in the past. This may be why they are attracting more young people who like the creativity and freedom. If this keeps them in the church—so be it! After all, Jesus preached wearing regular clothing, which included sandals on his feet.

About Living the "Mayberry" Way?

Pastors are continually looking for ways to keep their flocks safely in the fold. But with the competition of the daily "soaps," talk shows like Jerry Springer, professional football and the like, the church is losing its bid for attention.

That is, except for one church in Huntsville, Alabama that conducts a lemonade and popcorn Bible study with reruns from *The Andy Griffith Show* as an example of living out the moral principles as set forth in the scriptures.

Along with Bible "verses" as a basis for discussion, this slow and easy TV sitcom—*The Andy Griffith Show* serves as the basis for discussion during this one-hour-a-week class which is "bursting at the seams" with a standing-room-only crowd that grew from 28 to over 84.

What would Jesus say about this method of church expansion?

Ponder . . .

I Timothy 4:8 (NIV)

. . . but godliness has value for all things, holding promise for both the present life and the life to come.

Jesus took advantage of every means possible to introduce the crowds to the Father. He used examples from man to the animal kingdom, the sky, the earth, and the sea—even to writing lessons in the sand. Perhaps Jesus would have enjoyed viewing *The Andy Griffith Show*.

If We Don't Put Him First?

Do you remember when you knelt at the altar of your church, or bowed your head, to accept Christ as your Savior? You'd become a "new creature in Christ." Your old lifestyle began to pass away and your desire was to serve Him completely.

But as the years went by, and you became self-sufficient, your prayer habits and the closeness you'd felt to Christ began to wane. You'd become caught up with the things of this world. Your priorities had put Him on the "back burner."

Then one day you realized how lonely you were without the closeness of the Savior. As you knelt in prayer you seemed to hear Him say, "I never left you . . . I was there all the time."

Think over . . .

HEBREWS 13:5 (KJV)
. . . I will never leave thee, nor forsake thee.

To follow the Lord is to make Him Lord of your life. With Him in control, your life will stay on track. This is what Jesus would do.

If the Computer Interferes with Marriage?

"My husband and I spend hours in computer chat rooms," admitted Sally to her friend Jennie. "He talks to several girls on a regular basis, and I talk to guys."

"What do you talk about?" asked Jeannie.

"All kinds of things—college, politics, movies, and other things of mutual interest."

"Do you ever talk about your relationship with your husband—any problems you may have?" returned Jeannie.

"Well, yes . . . on occasion."

"Don't you think that can be risky—especially when you are talking to strangers?"

"Perhaps so—but I feel like I know each one personally . . . we've been communicating ever since my husband and I purchased the computer."

"Sally," said Jeannie in earnest, "please be careful!"

Think . . .

MARK 14:38 (NIV)
Watch and pray so that you will not fall into temptation. The spirit is willing, but the body is weak.

Making new friends is an enjoyable experience, especially when you have been formally introduced to them. This gives the relationship a firm ground on which to grow. However, making friends on the Internet should be done with extreme caution. One must be careful when giving out personal information, such as your name, address and telephone number to strangers.

And, constant communication breeds familiarity, which can cause a breakdown in one's defenses.

The Internet is a wonderful invention—but when it is misused it can lead to broken homes or life-threatening relationships. Jesus would admonish us to watch our steps—that we do not enter into temptation.

If You Face Breast Cancer?

Laura's family has always been concerned about breast cancer—her husband's mother died of it at age 55. Laura's mother had it at 82, and Laura had it at 58. Now, Laura's daughter has a suspicious lump in her breast.

Laura tells us that in the midst of her experience with breast cancer she learned how to replace fear with love and forgiveness, "My help comes from the Lord. I know I can't change my daughter's circumstances, but I can be there to love and support her and do what I can to help find the cause of cancer. Most of all, I can pray for those who face this challenge."

Envision . . .

PSALM 121:2 (NIV)

My help comes from the LORD, the Maker of heaven and earth.

It seems that certain illnesses attack certain families with a devilish force. However, our Lord has power over these forces and can restore health to those who have been through the valley of suffering. Our God will raise up the sick and restore them to health.

For Those of Little Faith?

"Have Faith In God!" says the pastor, "keep trusting in His Word."

However, while most of us have faith that the switch will turn on the light, and the key will cause the automobile to run, we, nevertheless, have difficulty trusting in the promises of God.

Since, without faith we cannot please God, we need to exercise faith by reading (and hearing) the Word of God. And when we pray, we must *believe* that we receive what we desire.

Listen to . . .

Mark 11:24 (NIV)
Therefore I tell you, whatever you ask for in prayer, believe that you have received it, and it will be yours.

Jesus would have us fight the good fight of faith, laying hold onto eternal life.

What Would Jesus Do for Women

If the Doctor is Late?

Did you ever wonder why you often have to wait a long time at the doctor's office? You may have thought to yourself, "Look at the clock—it's 3:00 PM and my appointment was for 2:00 PM. I've waited here for over an hour and it's still not my turn—I wonder if the doctor was out playing golf earlier and got back late? And after all that money that doctors earn, not to mention the high lifestyle that they live. It's not fair!

But have you considered that there probably is a valid reason why the doctor is running late? An emergency at the hospital—perhaps a patient took a turn for the worse. Or the doctor was very busy in his office.

Think about it . . .

II PETER 1:7 (NIV)

. . . and to godliness, brotherly kindness; and to brotherly kindness, love.

Physicians are often called away due to emergencies. Not only those waiting in the physician's office are inconvenienced but also those of his or her own family. Dinner is often eaten cold or not at all. Their children have already gone to bed and miss seeing their parent. As one young son of a physician said, "I don't want to be a doctor when I grow up—they never see their family!" Be understanding of your physician.

If We Are Ashamed of Him?

Jimmy was a high school student and a committed Christian. However, there was one problem—he wanted to share his faith with others around him but he faced a roadblock that prohibited him. It seemed his mind was bombarded with all kinds of fears, "What will people think of me? Will they see me as a religious fanatic or intolerant and narrow-minded?"

We are living in a world that believes that all faiths are equal. As a result, anyone who speaks out for the Lord is seen as narrow-minded and intolerant. What should Jimmy do?

Determine . . .

ROMANS 1:16 (NIV)

I am not ashamed of the gospel, because it is the power of God for the salvation of everyone who believes: first for the Jew, then for the Gentile.

Through meaningful soul-searching and prayer, Jimmy came to realize that his problem was from a fear of rejection. He spoke to his youth pastor and through reading the Bible and prayer, Jimmy was set free of the fear of rejection. Later, he became an outstanding witness for the Lord.

With a Committed Woman?

Most people realize that when someone, especially a woman, experiences spiritual renewal, there is no stopping her from "spreading the word." Everywhere she goes she tells others about God's love and enlists them to do the same.

Or it may be another cause, such as a "weight-loss" program where she has lost a considerable number of pounds. Not only does she tell others of her miracle, the weight-loss leaders set her up to do interviews to encourage others to enter the program. She is a committed woman! A woman who is committed to the cause of Christ brings pleasure to the heart of God.

Ponder . . .

PSALM 32:8 (NIV)
I will instruct you and teach you in the way you should go; I will counsel you and watch over you.

Do you lack purpose and commitment? Get into the Word of God, make friends with others who are also committed, and you will see a change in your life. This is what Jesus would do!

With a Talented Woman?

Betsy Ann began to keep time with music from when she was a very little girl. She would sing along with the tapes her mother would play for her.

"Yes, Jesus loves me," she would sing out with her baby-like voice. And after she was able to walk and move freely she would twirl around the room like a little ballerina.

"Betsy is so talented," remarked Mrs. Johnson to Betsy's mother, Mary, "I wonder if she will become a musician and dance or play the piano like you when she grows up."

"If that is her 'calling' it will be fine with me," responded Mary. "You know how much her father and I like music. We'd be pleased if she became a musician."

Meditate . . .

PSALM 18:49 (NIV)
Therefore I will praise you among the nations, O LORD;
I will sing praises to your name.

Our Lord has given each one of us a talent that needs to be developed for His honor and glory. While you may think that you have no talent, you may be surprised. It may not be in music, but is a talent nonetheless. Make it a point to discover what your talent is—writing, quilt-making, it's up to you to decide. That is what Jesus would tell you to do.

To Encourage Respect in Marriage?

"Have you met my wife?" asked Harvey enthusiastically, "She's the greatest!"

I shall never forget those words spoken by a man who seemed to love and respect his wife. From the way he said those words there was no doubt about it—he *was* in love!

But then look at Greg, who holds every other woman above his wife Jennifer. Greg rarely says a loving word about Jennifer. No wonder she has become depressed and is losing interest in life. She feels unloved and rejected.

Does marriage have to be like that of Greg and Jennifer? Does a difficult day at work mean that you go home and take it out on your spouse?

Consider . . .

PROVERBS 5:18 (NIV)

May your fountain be blessed, and may you rejoice in the wife of your youth.

Look at each other in a positive way. A difficult day at work does not mean that you go home and take your frustration out on your spouse. Perhaps he or she, too, had a rough day at work. By monitoring the other's mood, and acting in a way that will be uplifting, you will find that your concern will be appreciated. Also, a little perfume can go a long way!

To Slow Down a Bit?

Why are we always in a "rush?" Why do we want everything in a "instant?"

An old saying is "hurry up and go slow!" But is "hurry up" the way to go?

It's not very easy these days to take life at a slower pace. From morning until evening we rush about. One might look in on a day in the life of a family and hear these words:

"Hurry, get up and get dressed!" "Hurry and eat your breakfast!" "Hurry on to school!" "Hurry and come to the supper table!" "Hurry and do the dishes!" "Hurry and get your homework finished!" "Hurry up to bed!"

Think about . . .

LUKE 2:49 (NIV)
"Why were you searching for me?" he asked. "Didn't you know I had to be in my Father's house?"

I doubt if Jesus rushed about doing his father's business. The Scripture says he went about *doing* his father's business. Not, he rushed about doing his father's business. Also, he knew when it was time to rest and pray and he retreated quietly away from the crowds. Shouldn't we do the same? Take time to rest a little. Don't rush!

About So-Called "Adult" Entertainment?

Drive around in almost any city or town today and you will pass businesses with signs that say: Adult Movies, Adult Videos, Adult Novelty Shop. But should a shop set up for the sale and rental of pornographic materials use the word "adult" to describe such an illicit profession?

Why should our children or young people be taught that when they grow up—become adults, they should partake of such devices?

What do you think . . .

Isaiah 55:7 (KJV)
Let the wicked forsake his way and the evil man his thoughts. Let him turn to the LORD, and he will have mercy on him, and to our God, for he will freely pardon.

Pornographic material has no place in the life of anyone—even a mature adult. Such is offensive to our Lord Jesus Christ. Our hearts and minds should be set on things that are pure—not on the lust of the world.

What Would Jesus Do for Women

If People Won't Get Involved?

We've all heard the saying, "Mind your own business is the best policy."

But there are times when to mind your own can be deadly. Take the case of Marlene, who was killed in her own home by her husband. Even though neighbors heard her cry for help, none of them would come to her rescue or call 911.

Another woman, named Dorothy, was attacked on a dark street by a deranged man. Dorothy's cry to call the police went unheeded. Later, a neighbor was heard to say, "She shouldn't have been walking alone on that dark street."

Where is our sense of concern for those in need? What if we were in the same situation? Would we want someone to come to our rescue?

I wonder . . .

LUKE 10:33 (NIV)

But a Samaritan, as he traveled, came where the man was; and when he saw him, he took pity on him.
Also see Luke 10:34, 35 (NIV)

While the attitude of our present day is to not get involved in a situation where we could be in danger, or our schedule interrupted, we, nonetheless, are to be our brother's keeper. If we can save someone from bodily harm, we should do it. That's the law and is what Jesus would do.

With a Giving Heart?

At holiday time—or anytime, Mary Jane is always doing things for others. It may be baking cookies for the women's shelter in town or fresh-baked bread for the elderly widower down the street—or an errand for an invalid woman from her church. This isn't all—her husband, Marvin, enjoys delivering the goodies Mary Jane bakes for people. Truly, this couple's hearts are motivated by love.

"Mom," remarked her married daughter Pam, "I don't know how you keep up with all the work you do. You are busier now than before you retired."

"Maybe so," smiled Mary Jane, "but I just *love* doing things to make people happy. To see the smiles on their faces fills my heart with joy!"

Realize . . .

MATTHEW 19:19 (NIV)
. . . . 'love your neighbor as yourself.'"

Some people seem to have a giving heart and enjoy serving others. Nothing is too much for them to do for another person. They'd rather *serve* than be served. This pleases the heart of God, for love was the reason He sent his Son to this earth.

With a Blind Heart?

"He beat you and you had to go to the hospital?" questioned the talk-show host.

"Yes," admitted the 20-year-old wife.

"This isn't the first time he beat you—and you still want to stay with him?"

"Yes . . . because I love him."

"But what about the children—have you realized how this will affect them?"

"Yes, but he promised he'd change—not let his temper get the best of him anymore."

Think about . . .

Jeremiah 5:21 (NIV)
Hear this, you foolish and senseless people, who have eyes but do not see, who have ears but do not hear:

"How terrible!" you may remark, "a young woman of 20 years putting up with such abuse—and what a shame to put the children through such turmoil in the home. Is this young woman *blind* to her circumstances?"

Yes, she is blinded to her circumstances. How do you think Jesus would respond to this situation? What advice would He give the wife? You decide what Jesus would do.

To Save a Woman's Dignity?

When God created Eve to be Adam's counterpart did He expect more than He got? Regardless, Eve was a far cry from some of today's stalwart women. Like it or not, First Lady Hillary Rodham Clinton has managed to "stand by her man" amidst everything from infidelity to possible impeachment. Her dignity and silence is easily her most eloquent speech. Is her claim true that her strong religious faith has seen her through a time that would try anyone's spiritual commitment? What would Jesus say to Hillary Rodham Clinton during such trials and tribulations? What would He do to save her dignity?

Be honest . . .

JOHN 16:33 (NIV)

*"I have told you these things, so that in me you may
have peace. In this world you will have trouble. But
take heart! I have overcome the world."*

It is clear to almost everyone that our First Lady Hillary
Rodham Clinton has faced more public humiliation than any
of her predecessors in the White House. Nevertheless, she does
not flinch—but holds her head high as she stands faithfully at
her husband's side.

To Help the Aged Minimize Mistakes?

"My age is catching up with me," complained elderly Mabel Storey. "I try to remember things but yet I keep forgetting."

"What kind of things do you forget?" asked her friend Louise.

"Oh, so many things—like rinsing out the sink after I've washed the dishes, or picking up my bobby pins from the bedroom floor. My daughter Jean gets so frustrated with me. Sometimes I wish I were back in my own home again—or at the worst—in a nursing home. At least in a nursing home they know what to expect from us old folks. They aren't surprised when we do dumb things."

"Now don't go pitying yourself, Mabel—the Lord is well aware of your human frailty. He made us the way we are," admonished Louise.

Pray about . . .

PSALM 6:2 (NIV)

Be merciful to me, LORD, for I am faint; O LORD,
heal me, for my bones are in agony.

So often the elderly are misunderstood by those of the younger generation. Try as they may, the elderly do forget things from time-to-time. Those who care for these older folks should go out of their way to be understanding and loving. This is what Jesus would do.

To Work Hard and Rest?

"If you keep working at your present pace, and don't take time to rest, you'll have a nervous breakdown!"

Have you ever said those words to someone close to you—someone whose mind is always "working," even when he or she is on vacation? The paperwork goes along on vacation and he (your husband) sits in the hotel or on the beach—*working.* His *mind* is not on vacation.

"But I have to have this work finished before the end of the month," he argues.

Try as you may, you cannot change another person's obsessions. Work has become his main priority in life. It has become an *addiction.* All you can do is be a support and . . .

Pray . . .

PSALM 116:7 (NIV)
Be at rest once more, O my soul, for the LORD has been good to you.

Perhaps, along with prayer, you might encourage your husband to take a short nap during the day—just after the beach and before dinner. Since he's been working while on the beach, a short nap may be welcomed. When at home he needs to find a place where he works to get alone and close his eyes for a while—short as it may be, it will do him a lot of good. Jesus would have us rest our mind and body.

On a Trip to the West Coast?

You decide you'd like to take a motor trip to the West Coast where you can make a few garage sale stops from time-to-time; take in the sights of the area; maybe visit the music capital of Branson, Missouri; enjoy the baths of Hot Springs, Arkansas; view the Grand Canyon, and Yellowstone National Park.

But, what would Jesus do if He were taking such a trip? Yes, he would take in the sights; but also stop along the way to visit churches where he would minister to the needs of the people.

Or what . . .

LUKE 14:23 (NIV)
Then the master told his servant, 'Go out to the roads and country lanes and make them come in, so that my house will be full.

Wherever Jesus went He would be about His Father's business. He would always "walk-the-walk," and "talk-the-talk!"

About Respect for Our Flag?

We all recognize that moving depiction during World War II of the servicemen struggling to raise the American flag on the Island of Iwo Jima. Just the sight of it brings tears to many eyes—to raise the flag in victory where so many men and women gave their lives is to confess love for our flag and country.

For many years Americans as a whole were proud of the stars and stripes. In school and at every related event, the *pledge of allegiance* was recited by those in attendance. Sadly, today there seems to be a dwindling in America of love for our flag. In fact, on occasion, certain citizens have defiantly set fire to this precious symbol of the United States of America. Something needs to be done to restore patriotism in America.

Ask . . .

REVELATIONS 21:24 (KJV)
And the nations of them which are saved shall walk in the light of it: and the kings of the earth do bring their glory and honour into it.

A nation is no better than its inhabitants; so if we walk in God's light we bless our nation and bring honor to it. Also, we are to respect those who are in authority over us. This is what Jesus would do.

About Credit-Card-Itis?

Do you have the habit of pulling out a credit card for almost all of your purchases? Do you own lots of credit cards? And is it difficult to get them paid off? Then you may be suffering from *credit-card-itis.* If so, you are not alone. There are many people in the same situation. They plan to pay off their credit cards on a monthly basis, but find that they are using too many cards and the bills are exorbitant. So they pay only the monthly "minimum" and interest charges are added to the balance.

Do you promise yourself that you are going to pay off your credit cards as soon as you can, but discover that it is almost impossible? You are downtown shopping and see something that you think you "must have" and there you go again.

Ponder . . .

PROVERBS 22:7 (NIV)
The rich rule over the poor, and the borrower is servant to the lender.

While one person wouldn't own a credit card and throws out any invitation to own one, the next person may own credit cards which he pays off each month—thus avoiding the high interest rate. But another person is the one with credit-card-itis, he or she is like a gambler who can't quit! One answer to this "condition" is to pay off all credit cards and then destroy them—perhaps by placing them into the oven and baking them together, as some have done.

If you have credit-card-itis determine that you will look to the Lord for the strength to resist its hold on your life. Perhaps a credit card is not for you.

If Our Money Comes before God?

Have you ever met a Christian who spoke often about money and his or her desire to attain it?

They may attend church on a regular basis and sing songs like "simply trusting." However, whether they realize it or not, their speech betrays them. They may brag about how little money they spend, and dress like they live meagerly (while stashing away large sums of money into a bank).

We know the story of the rich young ruler whose faith, trust and heart were not in the right place. He trusted in himself and his ability to make money for his future. He was self-sufficient and self-indulgent. He was not unlike those of our culture today.

Contemplate . . .

Luke 12:29-31 (NIV)

*And do not set your heart on what you will eat or drink;
do not worry about it.*

*For the pagan world runs after all such things, and
your Father knows that you need them.*

*But seek his kingdom, and these things will be given to
you as well.*

It is not a sin to have money or riches, but it is a sin to *love* money and to put it ahead of service to our fellowman. Jesus said more about riches or lack thereof than almost any other subject. The story of the rich young ruler is one of many examples our Lord used to teach us that we cannot serve both God and riches.

If the Host Doesn't Pay?

"Ann, you and your husband have been going through a difficult financial time lately. Harry and I would like to take you both out to eat," said friend Yvonne Carter.

"Thank you," said Ann, "but let me check with Bobby first."

"OK."

Saturday evening went fine and the food was delicious. But then the check came.

Yvonne's husband picked up the check and studied it, then laid it on the table.

SILENCE!

Fully expecting that the Carters intended to pay for all four meals, yet trying to be polite, Ann nervously said to her husband who was seated next to Mr. Carter, "How much is our part?"

This was a mistake, because it opened a door that should have been left closed. You guessed it! Ann and her husband had to pay for their dinners. Now, on top of all their expenses they had another bill to pay. Their hearts SANK!

Think about it . . .

PSALM 85:10 (NIV)

*Love and faithfulness meet together; righteousness and
peace kiss each other.*

When invited out to dinner, unless it is specified as otherwise, you are a guest of the other party and they should pay for your meal. When Mr. Carter hesitated while looking at the check, then laid it on the table, Ann Johnson became embarrassed and spoke up. This took Mr. Carter off the hook. (Unfortunately, while the invitation was extended by his wife, she said nothing.) Consequently, the Johnsons had to pay for their dinners.

To Teach Our Children?

"How Big?" asks his father, and little Danny stretches his arms into the air. "That's a good boy!"

"How old are you?" questions Danny's mother.

With this, a little index finger is held up to signify that Danny is one year old.

Both parents clap their hands in excitement as Danny shows them what he has learned.

Our children learn by watching us. In fact, they are our greatest imitators. That's why it is important for us to be the best role models we can be.

Consider . . .

PSALM 27:11 (KJV)
*Teach me thy way, O LORD, and lead me in a plain
path. . . .*

It is alarming to see how many homes are filled with bickering and fighting. This is not the way to be a role model for our children. This kind of behavior "begets" (passes on) the same kind of behavior in our children. But joy and kindness teaches the same to the little ones. Ask yourself, what kind of behavior would Jesus exhibit? Love, Joy, and Peace, of course. This would please the Father.

To Say Thank You?

In spite of all the turmoil and hatred in this world, there are people who have love for others. One young woman had an experience that will bear this out.

It was the week of Thanksgiving 1998, when Jeannie was in line at the grocery store. Her car was full of the usual holiday food supplies—cranberry sauce, sweet potatoes, corn, bread crumbs, squash, turkey, and pumpkin pie.

As Jeannie opened her wallet to get the money out for her groceries a lady standing behind her in line leaned forward and said, "Put your money away—I'm going to pay for your groceries."

"Oh, no!" replied Jeannie with surprise, "I can't let you do that."

Jeannie's face put on a look of disbelief as the lady handed the money to the clerk.

"But I want to do it," explained the lady—"Happy Thanksgiving!"

Guess . . .

JOHN 13:34 (NIV)

*A new command I give you: Love one another. As I
have loved you, so you must love one another.*

Knowing that there are caring people in this world, Jesus
would bless the lady who paid her bill and then admonish
Jeannie to go out and spread the love she received to others—
not necessarily in the same way, but the way Jesus leads.

About Life in a Small Town?

Small town people are an interesting lot. *Nice 'n' Easy* is their motto.

In a small town the car in front of you comes to a *dead stop* while the driver, oblivious to anyone following behind, engages in a friendly chat with his neighbors.

In a small town the sound of your automobile horn is an unheard of disturbance—so you wait until the car moves on.

In a small town you have to ask for the *bill* when a serviceman (plumber, electrician, etc.) leaves your house.

"I'll stop by later," he may say as you wave your checkbook in the air, "no rush."

In a small town a freshly-baked cherry pie is delivered to your door by a smiling neighbor dressed in a brightly-colored apron.

"I never made you a pie when you moved in last month—so here it is—a little late," she apologizes.

All of these situations bespeak the *hometown* atmosphere.

Consider . . .

Matthew 10:11 (NIV)

Whatever town or village you enter, search for some worthy person there and stay at his house until you leave.

Jesus was an extraordinary man who lived an ordinary life in an ordinary town. In his day a traveler was welcomed into a home where he was fed and given a bed on which to sleep. In Jesus' small town of Nazareth, He would show hospitality just like his friends and neighbors.

If a Woman Won't Dress for Her Age?

Deep lines and wrinkles were visible on her elderly face, despite the orange-red dabs of rouge and matching lipstick that she wore. Her purple skintight dress, with a low neckline, revealed her almost bare flat chest. Two spindly legs wobbled on a pair of too-high heels. An over abundance of gaudy jewelry, with rings on every finger, made this matron's wardrobe complete.

"Yuk!" said Janice.

"Yuk!" agreed Patsy, "Why doesn't that woman dress for her age?"

"Beats me! Who is she trying to kid?"

Her head held high with confidence that she looked "gorgeous," the matron lady walked on by.

Decide . . .

I Peter 3:3 (NIV)
*Your beauty should not come from outward adornment,
such as braided hair and the wearing of gold jewelry
and fine clothes.*

A woman who dresses too young for her age is to be pitied—not criticized. Perhaps what she sees in the mirror is a much younger woman—not an elderly one. Or, she may think that to dress younger is to look younger.

Although the years have taken away her youth, this lady needn't be unattractive. Someone close to her could gently guide her in makeup application (most department stores have makeup counters where clerks would be eager to assist her). The dress department would help her choose clothes to "enhance" her age—not reveal it. Isn't this what Jesus would do?

What Would Jesus Do for Women

About Gossip?

What do too many women talk about when they get together—you guessed it . . . other women.

Unlike men, who like to talk about sports, business or on occasion women, some of the fairer sex like to talk about everything from hairdos, to diets, to poking fun at another woman's personal life—namely gossip!

Walk into a restaurant on a busy afternoon and you may see several tables of women busily engaged in gossip about who has left whom, or who is getting a divorce. Why do some women like to gossip more than men? Is this the proper way to act?

Think about . . .

PROVERBS 20:19 (NIV)

A gossip betrays a confidence; so avoid a man who talks too much.

Perhaps gossip comes from not having enough important things to fill our minds. Or that our world is too small. Perhaps it may be a fear of the failure of our own marriage. Nevertheless, Jesus would encourage us to fill our minds with the Word of God—not gossip.

To Beautify His Child?

Gucci, Versace, and Calvin Klein are designers of high-priced clothing fashions for which wealthy women and men spend millions of dollars each year. Then, there is the perfume industry with its hundreds of scents to spray on the body in order to create a pleasant odor. The cosmetic industry is another million-dollar endeavor that drains the finances of those of less income. Turn on the TV, and you'll see frequent advertisements for perfumes and cosmetics, hair care, and other products in an attempt to cleanse or adorn the body.

But, laying aside the millions of dollars being spent on medical and nutritional products in an attempt to heal the body, how much time and money is being spent to beautify the inner man—the spirit and soul of man? Very little, I'm afraid.

Meditate . . .

COLOSSIANS 3:12 (NIV)
Therefore, as God's chosen people, holy and dearly loved, clothe yourselves with compassion, kindness, humility, gentleness and patience.

God speaks in the book of Colossians with regard to the clothes for the inner man: compassion, kindness, humility, gentleness, patience, and forgiveness—all of which should be united in love. These are clothes that will beautify the child of God!

To Make Dreams Come True?

Harvey and Gladys worked hard all their lives and saved money to take a trip after they retire. Now that time has come—but Gladys is too ill to travel.

Leonard and Audrey worked hard all their lives and saved money to travel after they retire. Now that time has come—but financial adversity struck and took all their money.

Carl and Julia, like the other two couples, saved money to travel after they retire. But they were too late—Just before Carl was to retire, he had a heart attack and died.

What could all three couples have done to avoid the crises they were to face at the time of retirement?

Consider . . .

MARK 6:31 (NIV)

. . .*Come with me by yourselves to a quiet place and get some rest."*

Everyone has dreams for the future, but it is often wise to make your dreams come true while you have your health. If you have saved enough money, it may be wise to take one or more dream vacations *before* you retire. (Most people, by the time they are reasonably up in years, have enough money and accumulated leave time from their jobs to take a few trips before they retire.) Don't put it off!

When He Says "Follow Me?"

Julie and her boyfriend Chad had broken their relationship. After dating for a year and a-half, Julie, a committed Christian, had done everything she could to win Chad to the Lord. But, he made it clear that he was not interested in "religion."

All week long, as Julie sat at her desk job, her mind would recall the weekends when she and Chad would be together. Now what was she to do? At age 26 it seemed that her chances to find a Christian man with good qualities like Chad were slim.

As Julie took her dilemma to the Lord in prayer the words, *Follow me,* began to sound over and over in her mind. "What does this mean?" she asked herself. "Is this the Lord speaking to me, or am I imagining things?"

Think about . . .

PSALM 32:8 (NIV)
I will instruct you and teach you in the way you should go; I will counsel you and watch over you.

When two people date each other, they usually are together on a regular basis. During this time there is conversation and closeness between the two. As time goes on, that closeness can grow into love. Julie and Chad had the ingredients for love—but because the two of them were not walking together "in Christ" there was something missing—thus the breakup of the relationship. Our Lord said that two people cannot walk together unless they are agreed.

The words, *Follow me,* were God's way of guiding Julie in the right direction for her life. All she needed was to listen. Through reading the Word and earnest prayer, Julie will learn to follow the leading of the Lord—whether or not that includes Chad.

What Would Jesus Do for Women

About Cigarette Smoking?

With today's public consciousness turned toward the danger surrounding tobacco smoking, not enough can be said about this potential killer. Yet, once the addiction gets hold of a person, it is like a noose around the neck.

Many adults can recall when there were little or no restrictions regarding tobacco smoking. And the sight of ashtrays, cigarettes, and lighters were a part of the decor of many homes. One could light up cigarettes, cigars, or pipes almost anywhere—in the office, public buildings, public transportation, and, of course, in the automobile and at home.

Family members, from babies on up, were exposed to this "second-hand smoke" that unknowingly would do damage to their health. It wasn't until recent years that manufacturers of cigarettes would, by law, be forced to put *warning* notices on each box of cigarettes.

I wonder . . .

ROMANS 8:21 (KJV)
Because the creature itself also shall be delivered from the bondage of corruption into the glorious liberty of the children of God.

Alarmingly, many of yesterday's smokers have graduated from cigarettes to their own respirator, along with frequent admission into the hospital and finally a move to the local cemetery or crematorium. What would Jesus do? Remind the smoker of the gravity of their habit? Or, pray without ceasing?

About Answers to Prayer?

Jesus never questioned the Father's will. He always knew that, when he prayed, God knew best—from his lessons on how to walk and talk the way of truth to judgment for man's sin.

God is a righteous God—his plans for his people are far above any that we could make for ourselves. That is why we must seek him in prayer and daily follow in his footsteps.

Ponder God's promises . . .

John 16:24 (KJV)
. . . ask, and ye shall receive, that your joy may be full.

Jesus shows us the way to answered prayer. If we pray in faith, believing; and walk-the-walk and talk-the-talk; the answer will come in due time.

With a "Napping" Woman?

"So what's wrong with taking a nap now and then?"

Mothers of babies often grab a short nap during the day while baby is sleeping. After all, her night is a series of getting out of bed to nurse and change the baby's diapers. A nap during the day is just what she needs.

Retired and semi-retired women and men are likely to nap on their "lounge chairs" some time during the day.

In some countries, businesses close for two hours or more to allow their employees time to take a rest. Public offices such as the post office are also closed during this time. Undoubtedly, employees are more effective when they are rested. (Perhaps we, in the United States, could take a lesson from this.)

"A fifteen or twenty-minute rest revives me to where I can work for a longer period of time," said one self-employed woman.

Think about . . .

GENESIS 18:4 (NIV)
*Let a little water be brought, and then you may all wash
your feet and rest under this tree.*

Our Lord saw the importance of resting the body. This why resting is spoken of often in the scriptures. Do you take time to rest your body now and then? If not, try it. You may discover that it is a great way to get through the day.

With the Physically Challenged?

We met husky, bandana-wearing Bill one evening as we were walking along the Bay in a Florida city. Bill's fully-equipped conversion van was parked facing the Bay. He was in his wheelchair preparing to enter the lift to the van when we struck up a conversation with him.

"I travel all over the United States alone in this van," said Bill when asked about his unusual mobility in spite of being in a wheelchair. Wheelchair-bound he was not, for Bill had become almost as self-sufficient as one who can walk.

"You travel alone?" I asked with surprise.

"Yes, with this van and wheelchair I am almost totally independent."

After saying goodby, Bill positioned himself on the lift and rode up into the van to the driver's seat.

As he drove away, Bill waved and called, "See you on my next time around."

Ponder . . .

WWJD?

MATTHEW 15:31 (NIV)

The people were amazed when they saw the mute speaking, the crippled made well, the lame walking and the blind seeing. And they praised the God of Israel.

It is amazing to see how some "physically challenged" people make the best of their circumstances. Take television and movie actor Christopher Reeves, for example. Since he became paralyzed, after suffering a serious neck injury while riding a horse, he has become a national symbol of one who will not be defeated—in spite of the odds against him. Like our new friend, Bill, actor Reeves has taken the lemons in his life and made lemonade.

To Make a Visitor Welcome?

"Stop by anytime," said Audrey to her friend Viola, "you're always welcome."

"Thanks, Audrey," replied Viola, "but I don't like to disturb you—I know how busy you are with your husband and five children."

"Don't let that bother you. I enjoy your company. However, please don't mind if I continue my chores for a while, then we'll sit down for a cup of tea before I prepare supper."

"That will be fine! I'll see you in about an hour."

Audrey is a far-cry from her neighbor down the street—Mrs. Connors is married to a successful engineer. Her two children are away at college, yet she rarely takes time to entertain her friends. Her usual excuse is, "Call before you come—to see if it's convenient. You know how busy I am."

Consider . . .

I PETER 4:9 (NIV)

Offer hospitality to one another without grumbling.

Jesus would have us be hospitable and willing to give time for a visit from a friend. The gift of time is greater than an unwelcome appointment.

When Grandma Misses Grandpa?

"She walks around the house like a dejected soul," confides Beverly about her widowed grandmother Sophie, "I wish we knew what to do for her, she's so lonely and misses grandpa so much."

"Have you thought of the day-care for the elderly program?" asked friend Jennifer, "It's not that expensive and they get to be with others of their own age for a few hours a day. Our neighbor goes to day-care and enjoys it a lot."

Within a week or so, arrangements were made to have grandma go to day-care a few days a week. Later, Beverly and Jennifer talk again—

"How's your grandma doing?" asked Jennifer.

"Great! She's become one of the day-care pianists and is making friends with others—she doesn't seem so lonely anymore. Thanks for suggesting it," said Beverly." Mom and I really appreciate it."

Ponder . . .

Psalm 92:14 (NIV)
They will still bear fruit in old age, they will stay fresh and green,

Taking care of the needs of the elderly means more than just feeding and clothing them and giving them a place to live. They need a social life and new friends of like kind. Jesus would agree!

When Grandma Grows Old?

Grandma is growing old. It seems just yesterday that she was an innocent young girl of 16 with long black hair and dark brown eyes. Her complexion was olive and her smile like a charm. Even though she was not yet allowed to date, all the boys eyed this pretty little lassie in her flowing dress of pink and blue voile.

Now the years have taken their toll. Grandma's body aches with arthritis and her eyes are clouded with cataracts.

"A mighty handsome lassie, sh'ware," smiles Grandpa proudly. "A mighty handsome lassie she be!"

Ponder . . .

PSALM 37:25 (NIV)

. . . I was young and now I am old, yet I have never seen the righteous forsaken or their children begging bread.

Age is a fact of life. But through the eyes of love (grandpa), grandma can be as a beautiful young woman of 16. Our Lord sees us, not with the imperfections of age, but as one whose youth will never fade.

About Moving to Florida?

"When we retire we're going to move to beautiful Florida—the Sunshine State."

How often have we heard people make these statements? But I wonder if they've thought about what they would do if:

1. They move to Florida and buy a house, but are unable to maintain it?

2. They move to Florida and one or both become ill—who will take care of them?

3. They move to Florida and one spouse dies? Distance from their grown children makes it extremely difficult in case of illness or death—in case of death the body is often taken back home for burial. It has been said that the "turnover" in Florida is, at the most, every ten years—when people either move away, or die in Florida.

Ponder . . .

PROVERBS 4:11, 12 (NIV)

I guide you in the way of wisdom and lead you along
straight paths.
When you walk, your steps will not be hampered; when
you run, you will not stumble.

Jesus would admonish the future retiree to consider all the aspects of a permanent move to Florida. Perhaps it would be wiser to spend some time in Florida (not only in the winter months) to see if you like living there. Our Lord has promised to guide us.

About a Happy Childhood?

Twelve-year-old Sally takes piano lessons, dance lessons, and voice lessons. She studies all day in school and has homework at night. Sally is so busy with study of one kind or another that she has little time for anything else . . . even play.

Eleven-year-old Rodney takes trumpet lessons, piano lessons, and self-defense lessons. He, too, is in school all day and has homework at night. Like Sally, Rodney is so busy with studies that he has little time for anything else . . . even play.

Sally and Rodney are not unlike many children of today who are so preoccupied with studies. They are being robbed of their birthright—childhood.

Think about . . .

Job 21:11 (NIV)
They send forth their children as a flock; their little ones dance about.

Too many obligations can be very stressful for anyone—even a child. Like all of us, they need time for unstructured activities or play that is challenging physically, mentally, and socially. Have you ever watched children on a playground when they are allowed to decide what their play will be? Some want to be part of a ball game—others will jump rope—still others will make up a game of their own. So long as they are playing safely and having fun it doesn't matter how "structured" the game is. Jesus would say, "Let the children play!"

About Children without Marriage?

How would you like your daughter to follow some movie stars' example of *having children without marriage*?

"It's fashionable," said one teenager to her mother, " look at Jodie Foster—she doesn't need to be married to have a child."

"It may be fashionable, but it's morally wrong," replied her mother. "That's one reason why our Lord set up the institution of marriage—so that a child would have two parents—not just one. It's a big responsibility and God planned that it be shared by a husband and wife."

Besides, a successful movie star like Jodie Foster doesn't have to worry about where the money will come from to support her out-of-marriage children and herself.

Think about it . . .

*Marriage should be honored by all, and the marriage
bed kept pure, for God will judge the adulterer and
all the sexually immoral.*

Starry-eyed teenagers fail to realize the responsibility of raising a child alone. As the mother in the story said, it is morally wrong, as well as a great financial (also physical and emotional) burden to have children outside of marriage. It is also very difficult for a teenage girl, especially one who is still in school, to have to work to support and care for herself and a child. Besides, children need daddies!

With a Foolish Heart?

Playing children sometimes wear the costume of a "clown." Other names for a clown are jokester, fool, silly-billy, jerk, dingbat, dumbbell, pushover. . . .

We all know grownups who can never be serious—they are always "playing the fool." It is impossible for them to settle down, or converse intelligently. Anything you say to them is blown way out of proportion by their foolish minds. Their mouths are often filled with off-color stories.

The message of the gospel of Jesus Christ is foolish to them.

Do you know someone like this? Do you often wonder what can be done to cure them of this foolish way of thinking? Do you think they can be helped or have you given up on them?

Ponder . . .

PROVERBS 10:23 (NIV)

. . . A fool finds pleasure in evil conduct, but a man of understanding delights in wisdom.

While it is difficult to communicate with the "clown," there are ways of settling him or her down.

Encourage him in times when he is serious and ignore him when he is "playing the fool." If he sees that you are not going to engage in foolish conversation or laugh at his off-color jokes he will stop telling them to you. "Talk-the-talk!"

With a Rebellious Child?

It's amazing how children within the same family differ—one may have a gentle disposition, another a moderate one, and still another will fit the description of a "rebellious child."

A rebellious child resists authority, is often moody, and throws a temper tantrum when things don't go his or her way. Whatever the parents do or say doesn't seem to work. The child seems to be unhappy about everything and isn't afraid to show it.

Kicking and screaming, both at home and in public places, is not at all strange to the rebellious child—who usually finds himself in a class or school for special children.

Decide . . .

Isaiah 30:1 (NIV)
"Woe to the obstinate children," declares the LORD, "to those who carry out plans that are not mine, forming an alliance, but not by my Spirit, heaping sin upon sin;

Prayer and counseling, coupled with an in-depth look into the root of the problem, is often an open door to getting help for the child. Isn't this what Jesus would do?

If Someone Is Opinionated?

Family gatherings can be great fun—especially at holiday time. But scrumptious meals and the resulting cleanup tasks put family members into close proximity with each other—and that can have its recourse.

Whether the subject is religion or politics, each person has his opinion—and some individuals are more forthright in expressing themselves than others.

Take Uncle Harry, for example. He is known for his outspokenness; he has a strong opinion about most any subject. Furthermore, he will not be put into a losing position. In fact, he can become downright obnoxious if he feels threatened. How should one like Uncle Harry be dealt with?

Pray about . . .

DEUTERONOMY 9:6 (NIV)
. . . for you are a stiff-necked people.

In order to avoid a family squabble, people like Uncle Harry should be handled with utmost caution. Knowing how opinionated he is, there is no use allowing things to get out of hand by challenging Uncle Harry's strong positions. Just hear him out, smile, and go on to another subject—one where most can agree. This is what Jesus would do.

If We Fall?

Have you observed a young child lately, one who is learning to walk?

She wobbles as she tries to hold onto a chair—only to reach for the table next to it. Chances are she'll lose her balance more than once and fall to the floor. She may get a bump and shed a few tears as she looks around the room to see if mother or father is noticing her plight. When she is confident that all is well, she will again try to pull herself up.

"She won't give up" you say, "she is determined to walk."

So it is in our adult life—when we fall down spiritually we can either stay down on the "floor" of failure or decide to pull ourselves up and try again—even though we may fall again.

Think . . .

PHILIPPIANS 3:14 (KJV)
I press toward the mark for the prize of the high calling of God in Christ Jesus.

Just as a parent has love and compassion for a child who is learning to walk, so our Lord Jesus looks upon us with love and compassion when we stumble and fall in our spiritual life. We may fall again and again until we take hold of God's promises and walk in faith and victory.

What Would Jesus Do for Women

With Women Who Keep Their Maiden Names?

"Not going to take your husband's name?" gasped Sophie with disbelief, "I never heard of such a thing!"

"Get with it!" admonished Gail to her women's club friend. "Lots of women these days are keeping their maiden name. I don't see anything wrong with it."

"But what name will the children use—their mother's, father's, or both names? If the husband is to be the head of the household, shouldn't the family use his name—wife included? I think keeping one's maiden name after marriage is *women's liberation* gone too far!" complained Sophie.

Consider . . .

GENESIS 3:16 (KJV)
.. . . and thy desire shall be to thy husband . . . .

While the subject of a woman keeping her maiden name is somewhat controversial, there are certain instances (such as that of a celebrity or professional figure) where the public recognizes a woman's maiden name, and to use another name would be confusing. However, some women today keep their maiden name and add their husband's name to it: Jean Yardley-Brown.

So far as to what Jesus would do is open for discussion. Perhaps He would look at the motive behind keeping one's maiden name. If it is only to show resistence or competition toward her husband, Jesus likely would oppose the retaining of the maiden name. What is your opinion?

About a Woman Who "Flaunts It?"

"If You've Got It—Flaunt It!" is a worldly expression that ignores a person's modesty.

"Well, why not?" is the question asked to anyone who disagrees.

One's outward appearance—a pretty face and figure, does not necessarily mean there is beauty on the *inside*. Inner beauty does not depend on this—it is something that comes from a Godly life, and not being preoccupied with oneself, but caring for others.

Some of the most beautiful people we know are those who are "givers," not "takers." They may make a casserole for their neighbor who has illness or a death in the family, or they may help an elderly person prepare for bed at night. Their faces may be "plain" and their figures "dumpy," but the love that flows from them toward others cannot be matched.

Think . . .

PSALM 29:2 (KJV)
Give unto the LORD the glory due unto his name;
worship the LORD in the beauty of holiness.

As we know from the Scriptures, Jesus rarely looked on the outside of a person—He looked on the inside—the heart. To "flaunt" oneself is immodest and draws out earthly lusts. We are told to worship the Lord in the beauty of holiness.

When a Mother-in-Law Won't Accept Her Son's Wife?

What do you do when a mother-in-law favors her daughters and their families over her son and his family?

"I'm the daughter-in-law who is always playing *second-fiddle* to my three sisters-in-law," complains Leslie. "Whenever they need a baby-sitter their parents are available. Most times when I need a sitter they are too busy with the daughters' children."

At family gatherings I am treated like a "guest"—not as a family member. If I ask to help with the kitchen duties after a meal I'm told by my mother-in-law, "Go sit down—the girls will help me."

Is there any hope that Leslie will ever be accepted into this family?

I wonder . . .

RUTH 3:1 (KJV)

Then Naomi her mother in law said unto her, "My daughter, shall I not seek rest for thee, that it may be well with thee?"

One hope that most young married women have is to be loved and accepted by their husband's family. The husband is proud of his wife and he wants his family to also be proud of her. The young wife can learn a lot from her mother-in-law who is older and wiser. When this doesn't happen, and the daughter-in-law is rejected by her mother-in-law, stress is put on the marriage. A mother-in-law and daughter-in-law can have a beautiful relationship. The story of Naomi and Ruth is a good example.

Jesus would treat this situation with utmost delicacy—using *love* as the powerful force behind the mother-in-law and daughter-in-law dilemma.

When a Daughter-in-Law Won't Accept Her Husband's Family?

"She's going to pull our son away from us," Mrs. Bradley remarked to her husband just after her son's wedding ceremony.

Ron and Heather had met at college. Although their upbringing was vastly different from each other's, their love, nevertheless, was true. But in the case of Heather, her love for Ron would not extend to Ron's family.

"Most times when we ask to visit (which is rare), it is not the right time," complains Ron's mother. "Social events—parties, picnics, vacations, etc. include Heather's family, but not ours. Telephone calls and letters are almost non-existent. Our grandchildren hardly know us. What can we do?"

Pray about . . .

WWJD?

Matthew 7:7 (KJV)
*Ask, and it shall be given you; seek, and ye shall find;
knock, and it shall be opened unto you:*

Mr. and Mrs. Bradley's story is an all-too-common one. Grand-parents can bring a wealth of love and wisdom to a young married couple. But when one is too selfish to want to share love with the spouse's family, heartache and sorrow follow. To Mr. and Mrs. Bradley, Jesus likely would say, "Be patient and love your daughter-in-law. Be open to accept any time you can to spend with your son and his family. Keep in close touch (via telephone calls and letters) with your grandchildren as well as their parents. Then trust God for the answer.

About Leaving Shoes at the Door

"Leave my shoes at the door?" objected one shocked guest at a house gathering. "How disgusting!"

But the trend of guests shedding shoes at the doorstep is becoming increasing popular—especially since many of today's homes are decorated with light or white furnishings—including the carpeting.

The Eastern (Asian) custom of walking around the house shoeless is fast becoming popular in the USA. While in some areas of this country it has always been customary to walk around the house barefoot, in other homes mud rooms and entrance halls are the place to leave your shoes before entering the home. Some homes even provide a basket of socks and slippers at the door for guests.

Do you think this custom of a "shoeless home" is going too far?

Ask yourself . . .

1 PETER 4:9 (NIV)

Offer hospitality to one another without grumbling.

As the Scripture says, we should offer hospitality to each other without complaining. But some guests are embarrassed when asked to remove their shoes before entering a house. Not only is it somewhat intimidating, for a woman wearing nylon hose to walk on wood floors (which often lead from the carpeted area of a home to the powder room), more often than not it means runners in the hose.

How do we handle such a situation? Perhaps it may be wise to slip a pair of soft, easy-to-carry slippers in your handbag or another bag in your car. If you have never been to the house before you will at least be prepared. After all, isn't this better than having the host or hostess wash your feet, as it was in Jesus' day? Concern for one another's feelings should be upmost in our minds. Isn't this what Jesus would do?

About Rainy-Day Patterns?

"It's raining, boys and girls," announced Miss Daisy, "so we'll each take a pattern and draw a picture."

Some of the children would moan because they couldn't go outside for play. But not me—I enjoyed the patterns so much that the sight of rain would mean I could draw and paint—big beautiful turkeys at Thanksgiving and Santa Claus and toys at Christmas time.

Perhaps grownups should have "rainy-day patterns,"—something enjoyable to do when "rain"—times of disappointment, come into their lives.

Do you have "rainy-day patterns?"

Think about it . . .

LEVITICUS 26:4 (NIV)

*. . . I will send you rain in its season, and the ground
will yield its crops and the trees of the field their fruit.*

To our Lord rain means that plants and trees will grow and fruit will break forth. Brooks and rivers will have plenty of water for fish to swim. What is your answer to a rainy day? Perhaps you need to find some "rainy-day" activities that will enrich your soul—such as reading God's Word.

When Grown Children Return to the "Nest?"

When Bill and Mary Jane sent their youngest son, John, off to college their tears were bittersweet. While they would miss John, dearly, his leaving also had its advantages—namely—one less person in the bathroom, no more late-night telephone calls to girls, having the keys to their own car, "discovering" each other again, and turning John's bedroom into a combination bedroom/sitting room where they could relax, watch TV, and enjoy the plants and flowers that soak up the morning sun.

Little did Bill and Mary Jane realize that, after four years of college, 20-year old John would return home while he takes his time looking for a job—which, in light of the demand for *experienced* computer programmers, could take a long time. What are parents to do when a child returns to the "nest"?

Decide . . .

I Timothy 3:4 (NIV)
He must manage his own family well and see that his children obey him with proper respect.

Adult children return home for a variety of reasons, such as financial problems or unemployment, divorce or some other failure. What would Jesus do when a grown child wants to return home to the "nest"? Surely, Jesus would open the door to the son and welcome him into the home again—for as long as it takes the son to find a way out of his difficult circumstances. However, returning to the home does not mean that there are no *rules of the house*. The son will have to be aware that some things have changed since he was a youth at home. He will need to respect any *new* rules of the house. This is what Jesus would do!

When Children Worry?

Is it fair to say that only adults worry? Of course not!

The truth is that children also worry or become anxious, and it is not something that parents should overlook. Children worry about a wide variety of things, including future events such as how will they do in school or in sports, a forthcoming piano recital, illness and a fear of dying.

But if a child becomes a constant worrier and worry interferes with his or her sleep or concentration at home, school or with friends, you may be facing a problem that needs counseling with a pastor or even other professional help.

Decide . . .

MARK 10:14 (NIV)

. . . Let the little children come to me, and do not hinder them, for the kingdom of God belongs to such as these.

When Jesus came into a town the crowds rushed to see him. While he listened intently to the men and women, he gently opened his arms to the children. When the adults tried to pull the children away Jesus instructed them to, *Let the children come to me. . . .*

For Someone in Distress?

"Being up in years, I am unable to be mobile like I was when I was younger. My main mode of transportation is my three-wheel, battery-operated cart. At about 4:00 P.M. one day last week, just after I'd been grocery shopping, something went wrong with my cart. I called to a kind lady to call 911 for me. Being frustrated due to my circumstances, I forgot to get the lady's name.

"It took only about fifteen minutes for help to come. One young policeman arrived but couldn't get my cart into his car trunk. He called another officer and the two of them quickly loaded the cart, along with my groceries, into the trunk. Then, they took cart, groceries, and me, safely to my home. A *thank you* was all the reward they would accept."

Find out . . .

PSALM 121:2 (KJV)
My help cometh from the LORD, which made heaven and earth.

How often have we been in a situation where we needed someone to come to our rescue. Just as the caring policemen came to the aid of the lady in need, so our Lord will help us.

What Would Jesus Do for Women

If a Mother Has to Say Goodbye?

I looked out the dining-room window as the four of them passed by—a mother, grandmother, and two young granddaughters named Wendy and Jeannie. They all were arriving at the home of our landlady, Mrs. Maddox, who, with her now deceased husband, had reared many children throughout the years. Wendy and Jeannie were about to join that list of children— their young mother, Nancy, was about to die from an illness that was ravaging her body.

"How heartbreaking!" I thought, as I watched the family and Mrs. Maddox talking outside the house. Then, they all went inside to see where the children would live.

"Lord, please help these dear children," I prayed. "To grow up without a mother, especially during the teen years, undoubtedly will be very difficult." But then I thought of the love they will receive from Mrs. Maddox, and my spirit became peaceful. For though she, herself, was now getting along in years, Mrs. Maddox would be a good mother for Wendy and Jeannie.

Think . . .

PSALM 23:4 (NIV)

*Even though I walk through the valley of the shadow
of death, I will fear no evil, for you are with me; your
rod and your staff, they comfort me.*

What would Jesus do to comfort Wendy and Jeannie? My
thought is that He would open his arms with compassion and
say, "Come to me, little ones. Let me hold you." Then He would
rock them back and forth until they are at peace.

NOTE: I am told that at the time of the young mother's death, her mother (the
grandmother), held her daughter in her arms and quietly rocked back and
forth until Nancy slipped away into eternity.

What Would Jesus Do for Women

About a Deceitful Heart?

Brad and Fran live next door to Fred and Sara. Brad will do almost anything for his neighbors—mow their lawn when they are away, pick up their newspaper, or whatever else needs immediate attention. However, there's one thing about Brad that detracts from all the other good things he does—he has a deceitful heart.

"How can Brad have a deceitful heart when he is so neighborly?" you may ask.

"Here's how."

Brad went to a well known home center to purchase two outdoor chairs for his patio. The only thing wrong was that Brad was sent three chairs but charged only for two.

"That's their mistake," boasted Brad, "if they didn't catch the mistake then that's their problem."

Another example of Brad's deceitfulness is with regards to his being given too much change from a store.

"I'm not running back to the store to return the money. Their loss is my gain!"

But . . .

JEREMIAH 17:9 (KJV)

The heart is deceitful above all things, and desperately wicked: who can know it?

To some people Brad is a "good guy." In the sight of God he is a *deceitful* man. The third chair that Brad was delivered was an honest mistake made by the home center. It was not Brad's to keep. It belonged to the store.

Being a good neighbor is one thing, but that does not take the place of *honesty*. A personal relationship to Jesus Christ is what Brad needs.

About an Alcoholic?

Alcohol destroys homes; often turning fathers into monsters, mothers into secret slaves to the bottle, and youths into lazy loafers.

While alcoholism is said to be a disease, the Word of God calls it the result of sin. A disease will not keep us from heaven, but alcoholism can lead to us to the destruction of body and soul.

Alcohol is believed to be the number one killer on the highways of this country. It temporarily impairs vision, reaction speed, and coordination, as well as numbs inhibitions and guilt. After a few drinks, alcohol can make a fool out of those of high social standing as well as those of poorer economics.

Pray about . . .

I CORINTHIANS 6:10 (NIV)

. . . nor thieves nor the greedy nor drunkards nor slanderers nor swindlers will inherit the kingdom of God.

Jesus would be the first to warn those who are slaves to alcohol. It permanently destroys brain cells and affects the heart and liver.

What Would Jesus Do for Women

With a Cheating Heart?

"He cheated on me, so I cheated on him!" admits one young woman on daytime TV.

Day-after-day the talk show hosts introduce a myriad of young men and women—mostly uneducated and under the age of 20, who are embroiled in illicit affairs.

Unfortunately, those who are most affected by these "cheating hearts" are the offspring—the children who are born out of these relationships. Not only are the children often deprived of a two-parent home, they are also deprived of many of the necessities of life. Father doesn't work, so the mother has to work or live on public assistance.

Make up your mind . . .

HEBREWS 13:4 (NIV)
*Marriage should be honored by all, and the marriage
bed kept pure, for God will judge the adulterer and
all the sexually immoral.*

"What would Jesus do about the cheating heart?" you may
ask. Would you agree that He would open His heart to them,
speak the words of Life, and encourage then to set their houses
in order?

With a Broken Heart?

"He died of a broken heart," rumored his friends,

It had been only six months earlier that 70 year-old John Filmore's wife, Jane, had passed away due to multiple health complications. John's grief was overwhelming—he would walk about his house, around the block and then downtown. Then he would repeat the same routine. On occasion, neighbors would provide him with a hot bowl of soup or casserole for his dinner.

They would often telephone to see how he was doing.

But John's broken heart seemed to be non-repairable. He'd lost the love of his life and the will to live. Then one day John's loneliness and grief gave way to death—he died of a broken heart!

Pray . . .

WWJD?

Psalm 31:9 (NIV)
Be merciful to me, O LORD, for I am in distress; my eyes grow weak with sorrow, my soul and my body with grief.

We've all known people who are lonely for one reason or another. While, like John Filmore, some are lonely as a result of the loss of a loved one, others are missing a child who is a long distance away at college, others are lonely because of a divorce . . . and the list goes on.

We should remember to pray for those who are hurting—that's what Jesus would do.

To Make the Most of Retirement?

"I never wanted to retire and sit on a creek bank or pull a golf buggy around. When you retire you should stop doin' one thing and start doin' another."

—Colonel Harland D. Sanders,
Founder of Kentucky Fried Chicken, Inc.

Unfortunately, too many retirees stop doing one thing (leave their life's work) only to sit around and do nothing—except for Uncle Walter.

"Why don't you take your hobby of photography and make slides of the hundreds of photographs you've taken over the years (from the mountains of Colorado to the glaciers of Alaska)? Then prepare a slide presentation for service clubs (Rotary, Lions, etc.)," suggested his sister-in-law Joan.

Uncle Walter did just that, and today, at age 79, his life is more complete than its ever been.

Ponder . . .

PROVERBS 12:14 (NIV)
*From the fruit of his lips a man is filled with good things
as surely as the work of his hands rewards him.*

Just like Colonel Sanders and Uncle Walter, our Lord Jesus
Christ never retired from the ministry He came to earth to do.
His hands never became idle. For as long as He was on this
earth Jesus continued to "walk-the-walk" and "talk-the-talk"!

What Would Jesus Do for Women

About Card Playing?

For many years card playing, with its "joker" card, has been associated with drinking in saloons. It was considered the "devil's" game! Committed Christians strongly opposed the game.

Colonel Harland Sanders of Kentucky Fried Chicken fame remembered that when he was little on up his mother warned him about card playing. "Son, stay away from cards, because card playing leads to gambling; gambling leads to shooting; and shooting leads to killing!"

If the Colonel Sanders' statement sounds "far-fetched," you may not be aware that the origin of card playing was the medieval *tarot card* (known today for fortune telling).

Today, playing cards are the most widely used objects of diversion in the world. Estimates suggest that more than three-quarters of all people play one or more types of card games. The elderly (especially retirees) are especially drawn toward card playing. Even some Christians now find card playing very compelling and play them on a regular basis. Who is the biggest *"joker"*?

Consider . . .

II Corinthians 6:17 (NIV)

Therefore come out from them and be separate, says the Lord. Touch no unclean thing, and I will receive you.

II Corinthians 7:1 (NIV)

Since we have these promises, dear friends, let us purify ourselves from everything that contaminates body and spirit, perfecting holiness out of reverence for God.

The subject of card playing very well may be one of the most controversial in this book. For this reason you should examine your heart and ask the Lord what to do about card playing. You also may wish to consider your testimony before the world.

There are many other games that can bring a lot of enjoyment. Let the Lord lead you to choose the right ones.

About Elderly Drivers?

"Did you know that the automobile death rate per 100,000 people (per the National Safety Council) has gone down for all age brackets except the elderly?" Bob asked his co-worker Jim.

"No, I didn't," replied Jim.

"It's double for those over age 75 than for the rest of us."

"Bad news!"

"Yes, and those over age 75 can send in a check to renew their drivers license for six years. They can even do it by telephone."

"Does that mean what I think it means?"

"Yep! More danger on the roads!"

Consider . . .

DEUTERONOMY 33:25 (KJV)
. . . and as thy days, so shall thy strength be.

What a difficult time in one's life—when age has become a liability and you are unable to be as mobile as you once were. Concern for an elderly relative or friend's safety can become monumental for those in charge of their care. As with all ages, Jesus was and is concerned about those who are up in years.

With an Unpredictable Heart?

The 20th century, like other centuries, can be remembered for everything from wars to peace negotiations, medical breakthroughs, as well as new illnesses for which there is yet no cure.

In spite of our new understanding regarding health and nutrition, there is one organ of the body whose failure to function properly is so widespread that it often needs surgical repair—that physical organ is called the "heart."

Despite the fact that it, too, is so unpredictable, the "spiritual" part of the heart (the "essence of man") can go off-course and act in a way that defies right living. This is also referred to as a "cheating heart," and in this 20th century this condition has affected some of the most powerful leaders of our nation—including our President.

What is the answer . . .

JEREMIAH 17:9 (KJV)
The heart is deceitful above all things, and desperately wicked: who can know it?

As the scripture says, "the heart is deceitful . . . ." With this knowledge we should guard the heart from sin, and make sure that our spiritual life is in tune with the Lord. The first step to healing a cheating heart is the confession of our sin to the Lord and rejection of that and other sins which may come into our lives.

About the Theater?

Jesus used many ways to spread the message of the gospel—one was when he knelt down and wrote in the sand. The *parable* (a fictitious story that illustrates a religious principle), told the truth with vivid descriptions that often pierced the hearts of those who heard him.

While mental pictures brought the truth to the mind's eye of people of Jesus' time, much of what is seen and heard at today's local movie theater is not fit for human consumption. Not only is immorality portrayed, there is a proliferation of profanity from frame to frame. PG rating used to mean that the movie is likely to be acceptable for everyone. Today, one cannot be sure that any movie in the local theater is acceptable.

Decide . . .

II Corinthians 6:17 (NIV)
"Therefore come out from them and be separate, says the Lord. Touch no unclean thing, and I will receive you."

While the majority of Christians of our earlier years refrained from attending the local movie theater, the entrance of television into society has brought with it an acceptance of the theater as a whole. With more and more immorality and profanity being portrayed on the screen, isn't it time for Christians to take action against movies that are billed as PG or PG13, yet contain unacceptable material? Or is it time for believers in Jesus Christ to return to the standards of yesteryear?

About Live-Wire Kids?

"What am I doing wrong?" Stephanie asked her neighbor, Jennie. "When my kids get home from school they are so tensed-up that they could almost climb the walls!"

"I can understand your problem," answered Jennie. Ever since our school board voted to do away with *school recess* the kids come home from school like 'live-wires.' They would rather play outside than eat their dinner. Then, when it's time to do homework they 'die-out!' I read recently that many educators see recess as an important component of a child's education. That unstructured free-for-all time, especially helps a child both physically and socially."

"Well, it's time we go to a school board meeting and make our voices be heard!"

"Agreed!"

Find out . . .

1 TIMOTHY 4:8 (NIV)
For physical training is of some value. . . .

In this day of *physical fitness*—especially for adults, it is wise to consider the same for our school kids. Sitting in front of a TV cannot benefit a child like play can do. Our Lord, in his Word, reminds us that *physical training* has its benefits. He should know, because he walked almost everywhere he went. Perhaps we, too, should walk more.

About the Unisex Generation?

During the early years of this century, novelist Grace Livingston Hill was in a class by herself. Her books like *Matched Pearls*, *Silver Wings*, and *Beauty for Ashes* introduced the reader to a world where ladies wore flowing feminine dresses and men wore suits with shirt and tie. "Cross-dressing" (women wearing men's clothes and men wearing women's clothes), was unheard of.

In comparison, in today's *unisex* generation one can hardly differentiate between men and women when both have the same short haircut, tailored pantsuits with shirt and tie and shoes similar in style to that of a man. What has happened to the feminine woman and the masculine man?

Consider . . .

GENESIS 6:19 (KJV)

*. . . of every living thing of all flesh, two of every sort
shalt thou bring into the ark, to keep them
alive with thee; they shall be male and female.*

God never intended for men and women to be alike. He created them male and female with a definite distinction between the two—each with individual appearances, each performing certain tasks. Isn't it time we get rid of the *unisex* look and ways and become two sexes as God created us?

About "Tattoos for the Lord?"

We all are familiar with the tattoos on the muscular arms of a sailor. Some of the tattoos are of a heart with the name of *a sweetheart* or *mother* inside; while others may exhibit the likeness of a scorpion.

Did you know that the book of Leviticus warns us not to cut our bodies for the dead or put tattoo marks on ourselves?

Yet, today there are those professing to be followers of Christ (calling themselves *evangelical Christians*) who put tattoo marks on their bodies as an expression of "extreme faith."

Extreme faith, indeed. This "extreme faith" as they call it, is none other than *apostasy*.

Isn't it amazing the way *unregenerate man* tries to change the scriptures to suit his own delusions? (Of course, they attempt to explain the warning in Leviticus with non-applicable scriptures.)

Decide . . .

LEVITICUS 19:28 (NIV)
*Do not cut your bodies for the dead or put tattoo marks
on yourselves. I am the LORD.*

Would you believe that in these *last days* people are returning to the heathen practices of the first centuries? Cutting the
flesh (earrings, nose rings, lip rings, as well as tattoo marks)
some all over the body. That's why we are told to guard our
faith so that no one takes it from us.

About a Career Put on Hold?

Mary Lou and Jeff met at college. Jeff was captain of the football team—Mary Lou a cheerleader. Both had high hopes for the future. Jeff was on the road to becoming a nuclear engineer, Mary Lou a nurse. Then one day it all changed.

"I'm pregnant, Jeff," confided Mary Lou.

"Oh, no!" moaned Jeff. "I can't marry you now—I've got to go on with my career."

Months later, Mary Lou became an unwed mother, with the responsibility of a job and a baby to raise alone.

Consider . . .

II Timothy 2:22 (NIV)

Flee the evil desires of youth, and pursue righteousness, faith, love and peace, along with those who call on the Lord out of a pure heart.

The story of Mary Lou and Jeff is an age-old one, but nonetheless tragic. While Jeff went on with his career, Mary Lou's dream of becoming a nurse was a long way off. Had the two of them refrained from having sex before marriage, the story might have ended on a happier note. Jesus wants couples to hold their standard high and respect the sanctity of marriage. Mary Lou made the best choice—keeping her baby. Her career plans were put on hold.

About an Abortion?

"Only tissue," the abortionists would call it—"not a real baby."

Sadly, these six words would be the death sentence to millions of babies.

With these six words in mind, "only tissue—not a real baby," young and unmarried Theresa would subject her body and her baby's body to a certain future. Death for her unborn child and guilt and shame for Theresa.

"The feelings of guilt will pass." said the pro-choice proclaimers—but it didn't—not for Theresa.

After weeks and months of mental and emotional torture, Theresa heard about God's forgiveness—that she can be forgiven of the sin of abortion and every sin she has ever committed—both known and unknown. Then, Theresa repented of her sins and became "clean" before God.

Consider . . .

Ephesians 1:7 (NIV)

In him we have redemption through his blood, the forgiveness of sins, in accordance with the riches of God's grace.

Jesus, and the Father rejoice when one sinner comes to repentance.

To Plan for Old Age?

Think you're too young to make plans for when you are old?—not so!

We hear so much today about *Financial Planning*. Why not plan for old age? After all, there are some points of wisdom that you should consider to prepare for this time in your life:

1. One floor living—such as a ranch-style house or an apartment or condo, if steps are a problem.
2. Exterior and interior lights with sensors that go on when it gets dark.
3. Wide doorways and a level entrance for wheelchair accessability.
4. A first floor shower with no ledge on the floor and with room for a chair.
5. Toilets installed high enough for easy access.
6. A kitchen designed for convenience and safety.
7. Nonskid floors and secure rugs and pads to prevent falls.
8. A convenient location where you can get about without driving a car.
9. Enough storage so you don't have to be crowded.

Consider . . .

PROVERBS 1:5 (KJV)
A wise man will hear, and will increase learning; and a man of understanding shall attain unto wise counsels:

Jesus taught us to be wise and productive in our everyday living. Would he not agree with the *nine points of wisdom* that we list here. After all, aging has always been a natural process of man—even in Jesus' day.

With a Wave and a Smile?

Have you ever driven through a small town and noticed older men in overalls sitting on benches around the "town square"? Others, especially husbands and wives, can be seen rocking on their front porches—just watching people and cars go by. Have you also noticed what a wave and a smile can do for them? In fact, most times a smile can turn a frown or dejected look into a smile in return.

Smiles should not be kept only for strangers—our friends, family and co-workers can use a smile once in a while. They are the most important people in your life. Shouldn't they get more smiles than the rest?

Ask yourself . . .

Job 9:27 (NIV)
If I say, 'I will forget my complaint, I will change my expression, and smile,'

Surely, Jesus brought many smiles and waves as he walked throughout the villages of His day. His presence, alone, would have changed frowns into smiles. It is His desire that we, too, put on a smile—and a happy heart. When have you turned a frown into a smile? It's easy! Try it. You'll like it!

About a Camera-Shy Woman?

"Don't take my picture! I look terrible!" said young Sandy with the clear smooth skin, glistening blonde hair, and tall slender body.

That was 55 years ago and now Sandy is an elderly woman who lives with her daughter Lucille. Now when Sandy looks at present-day photographs of herself she sees an aged woman with lines on her face and white hair on her head.

Why is it that when we are young we don't appreciate our youthful appearance—we take it for granted? But when we are old we think back to those days and wish we could only look like that again.

Ponder . . .

PSALM 71:18 (NIV)
Even when I am old and gray, do not forsake me, O
God, till I declare your power to the next generation,
your might to all who are to come.

Whether young or old, life was intended to be lived to the fullest—not as a day-by-day humdrum experience. God intended that we face each day with excitement and joy for the challenges He sets before us.